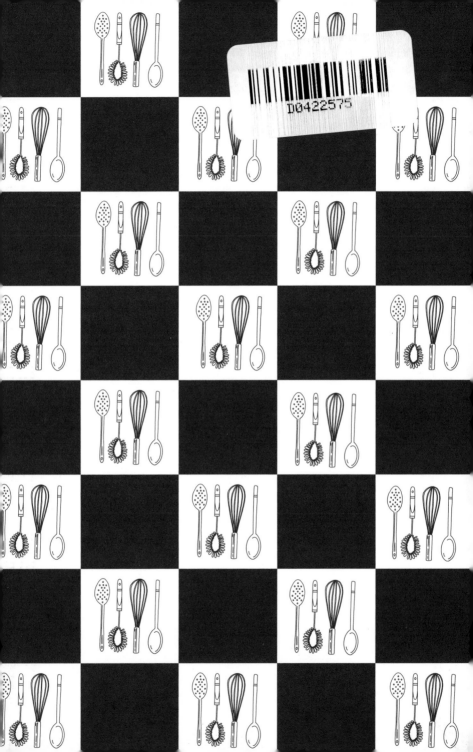

PASTA
SAUCES

Consultant Editor:
Valerie Ferguson

southwater

Contents

Introduction

The recipes in this book show that pasta sauces are almost limitless in their variety, as are the pasta shapes served with them. Sauces can be quick and simple or more elaborate and luxurious, using all kinds of vegetables and herbs, fish and shellfish, chicken and meat. They can make the most of seasonal fresh ingredients or marry together a few items from the store cupboard to create a tempting meal.

Both regional Italian and Sicilian dishes are featured, including such classics as Bolognese Sauce with Tagliatelle and Alfredo's Fettuccine. You will also find modern recipes such as Sun-dried Tomatoes & Radicchio with Paglia e Fieno. Whether you want a speedy midweek meal or are looking for inspiration for entertaining, you will find just what you need within these pages. Enjoy a Fresh Tomato Sauce that is simplicity itself to make; indulge in creamy Chicken, Broccoli & Cheese with Penne; or really push the boat out for a dinner party with Lobster with Capelli d'Angelo, a sophisticated dish with a rich flavour.

Use this book to build up your repertoire of delicious pasta sauces and you will always have the perfect meal solution at your fingertips whatever the season or occasion.

Ingredients

The best Italian pasta sauces are based on fresh seasonal produce and creative use of store-cupboard ingredients.

Fish & Shellfish

Many pasta sauces use fresh fish and shellfish. Fresh salmon, prawns (shrimp), clams, mussels and lobster all feature in the recipes in this book, as do canned tuna and anchovies and smoked salmon.

Prawns

Clams

Poultry & Meat

Chicken is a popular ingredient of pasta sauces – breast fillets are quick to cook. Minced pork and beef are used in more slowly cooked sauces; beef is required for the famous Bolognese Sauce. Meaty, highly seasoned fresh sausages make quick sauces. Cured meats such as bresàola (beef) and prosciutto crudo (Parma ham), as well as sausages like salami, have an important role to play. Pancetta (Italian streaky (fatty) bacon) is used to add flavour to sauces; if unavailable, it may be substituted with ordinary smoked streaky bacon.

Italian sausages

Pancetta

Vegetables

A huge range of fresh vegetables is used, including asparagus, aubergines (eggplant), broccoli, carrots,

Asparagus

cavolo nero (Tuscan black cabbage, a close relative of curly kale), courgettes, (zucchini) fennel, French beans, globe artichokes, leeks, mushrooms (wild and cultivated, fresh and dried, such as porcini), onions and spring onions (scallions), peppers, and radicchio. Tomatoes are probably the most ubiquitous ingredient in pasta sauces, particularly the Italian plum variety, whether fresh, canned whole or chopped, as passata (strained pulped tomatoes), or sun-dried in olive oil or as tomato purée or paste.

Porcini

Peppers

Tomatoes

Dairy Produce

Italy produces wonderful cheeses. Gorgonzola is a creamy blue. Mascarpone is a rich, triple-cream cheese with a mild flavour. Mozzarella, a fresh, white, mild cheese, is made from water buffalo's or, more commonly, cow's milk. Parmesan, long-aged and with a wonderful taste, is invaluable for adding flavour to pasta sauces: always buy it in a piece and grate freshly as

Parmesan

needed. Pecorino is a salted, sharp-tasting cheese made from ewe's milk. Ricotta is a very soft, white cheese with a bland flavour that combines well with strong-tasting ingredients. Ricotta salata is a salted and dried version of ricotta that can be diced,

Ricotta   crumbled and even grated. Creamy pasta sauces may call for single (light) or double (heavy) cream, *panna da cucina* (cream for cooking – a long-life product to keep in the store cupboard), or crème fraîche. Milk, butter and eggs also feature regularly in pasta sauces.

Nuts, Herbs & Spices

Pine nuts, small and creamy-coloured, are an essential ingredient of pesto sauce. Walnuts combine stunningly with Gorgonzola and mascarpone cheeses to make one of the speediest pasta sauces.

Walnuts   Both fresh and dried herbs are used in abundance to flavour pasta sauces. Basil, one of the most popular, is best used fresh as it loses much of its character when dried. It is the perfect complement to tomatoes. Garlic enlivens many sauces: Italian cooking tends to *Garlic* use it with discretion so that it enhances without flavouring too aggressively.

Chervil, chives, dill, flat-leaf parsley, marjoram, oregano, rosemary, sage, tarragon and thyme all add their

distinctive qualities to sauces. Red chillies, fresh or dried (whole or crushed), or chilli sauce

Oregano may be used   *Red chillies* to give heat and spiciness to sauces such as *arrabbiata*. Nutmeg brings a rich, musky flavour to white sauces. Saffron, though expensive,   *Saffron* imparts a wonderful aroma and colour.

Seasonings & Flavourings

Olive oil, with its distinctive flavour, is widely used in cooking pasta sauces. There are various grades: for cooking, pure and virgin oils are fine; extra virgin, the highest quality, is best reserved for using raw and in dressings.

Balsamic vinegar, rich, dark and mellow, can add a slight sharpness to sauces. Choose one that has been aged for at least 12 years if possible. Red and white   *Balsamic* wine, sparkling white wine,   *vinegar* vermouth and even vodka are used to give richness and an extra kick.

Black and green olives, preserved in oil or brine, are good in strongly   *Black olives* flavoured sauces.

Capers, the flower buds of a Mediterranean shrub, often preserved in brine, bring a piquant, peppery flavour to seafood sauces.

Types of Pasta

Make the most of any pasta sauce by choosing the appropriate type of pasta to accompany it from the many shapes and flavours available.

Most pasta is made from durum wheat flour, which is quite hard and does not go soggy when cooked. Dried pasta may simply have been mixed with water or may also contain egg, while fresh pasta – *pasta all'uova* – always contains egg. As a result of a growing interest in healthy foods, wholewheat pasta, which has a rich brown colour, has become increasingly popular. Buckwheat pasta, which is even darker, is also available and is suitable for people on a gluten-free diet.

Pasta may be coloured and flavoured with a range of ingredients. The most common additions are tomatoes and spinach, but beetroot, saffron, herbs, and squid or cuttlefish ink are also widely used.

There are no hard-and-fast rules about which shapes to serve with particular sauces, but some shapes do work better than others. The recipes in this book include a recommendation, described in the list below, but you can substitute a shape of your choice.

Capelli d'angelo take the form of very fine, long strands and are good with delicate-tasting seafood sauces.

Cappelletti are small, round, filled shapes that go well with a simple sauce like tomato and basil that complements their filling.

Cappelletti

Eliche are short twists of pasta.
Farfalle, shaped like butterflies or bows, are excellent with shellfish and meat and in cold pasta salads.

Farfalle

Fettuccine are long, narrowish ribbons that go well with creamy sauces.
Fusilli are short spirals that make a good partner to tomato and vegetable sauces.

Fusilli

Garganelli, which are narrower tubes than rigatoni, are good for 'holding' thick sauces.
Linguine are long strands.
Paglia e fieno, 'hay and straw', are a type of long, broad or narrow noodle.

Paglia e fieno

Penne are ridged, short tubes cut diagonally.
Pipe rigate, 'ridged pipes', are very good with thick, chunky sauces.

Pipe rigate

Rigatoni are short, ridged tubes of medium diameter which are excellent with sauces containing meat.
Spaghetti, the best-known pasta, take the form of long strands with a circular cross-section.
Tagliatelle are long, flat, noodles made with egg.
Trenette are another form of narrow, long-stranded pasta.

Tagliatelle

Techniques

Making your own pasta is very satisfying. With a little practice you can experiment with different flavours and shapes.

Basic Pasta Dough

Serves 3–4

INGREDIENTS
200 g/7 oz/1¾ cups plain (all-purpose) flour
    (Italian tipo 00 is the best. You can
    find it in Italian delicatessens)
pinch of salt
2 eggs
10 ml/2 tsp cold water

Making Pasta by Hand

1 Sift the flour and salt on to a work surface and make a well in the centre. Put the eggs and water into the well. Using a fork, beat the eggs together, then draw in the flour from the sides, combining to make a thick pasta.

2 When the mixture becomes stiff, use your hands to combine to a firm dough. Knead for about 5 minutes.

3 Wrap the dough in clear film (plastic wrap) and rest for 30 minutes.

Making Pasta in a Food Processor

1 Sift the flour into the bowl of the food processor and add a pinch of salt. Beat the eggs with the water and pour into the flour.

2 Process until the dough begins to come together. Tip it out on to a lightly floured surface and knead until smooth. Wrap in clear film and leave to rest for 30 minutes.

Cooking Pasta

1 Tip the pasta into a large pan of salted boiling water. Stir once to prevent sticking. Do not cover. Quickly bring the water back to a rolling boil and boil according to the packet instructions until *al dente* (just firm to the bite).

2 Drain using a large colander or sieve (strainer). Rinse with boiling water to prevent the pasta sticking. If the pasta is to be eaten hot, serve immediately with your chosen sauce.

Easy Tomato, Wine & Cream Sauce

Tomatoes, cream and fresh basil are a truly winning combination.

Serves 4–6

INGREDIENTS
400 ml/14 fl oz/1⅔ cups passata
90 ml/6 tbsp dry white wine
150 ml/¼ pint/⅔ cup double (heavy) cream
225 g/8 oz/2 cups fresh cappelletti
1 small handful fresh basil leaves
60 ml/4 tbsp grated Parmesan cheese
salt and ground black pepper

1 Pour the passata and wine into a medium saucepan and stir to mix. Bring to the boil over a medium heat, then add the cream and stir until evenly mixed and bubbling. Turn the heat down to low and leave to simmer gently.

2 Cook the pasta in salted boiling water according to the instructions on the packet until *al dente*. Meanwhile, finely shred most of the basil leaves and set aside with the whole leaves.

3 Drain the pasta well, return it to the pan and toss with the grated Parmesan. Taste the sauce for seasoning, pour it over the pasta and toss well. Serve immediately, sprinkled with the shredded and whole basil leaves.

COOK'S TIP: This sauce can be made up to a day ahead. Reheat gently in a heavy-based saucepan while the pasta is cooking.

Tomato & Balsamic Vinegar Sauce with Fusilli

The intense flavour of balsamic vinegar gives a pleasant kick to this sauce.

Serves 6–8

INGREDIENTS

2 x 400 g/14 oz cans chopped Italian
   plum tomatoes
2 pieces drained sun-dried tomato in
   olive oil, thinly sliced
2 garlic cloves, crushed
45 ml/3 tbsp olive oil
5 ml/1 tsp granulated sugar
350 g/12 oz/3 cups fresh or
   dried fusilli
45 ml/3 tbsp balsamic vinegar
salt and ground black pepper
coarsely shaved Pecorino cheese and
   rocket salad, to serve

1 Put the first five ingredients in a pan. Season to taste. Bring to the boil, stirring. Lower the heat and simmer for about 20 minutes until reduced.

2 Meanwhile, cook the pasta in salted boiling water according to the instructions on the packet until *al dente*.

3 Stir the vinegar into the sauce. Cook for 1–2 minutes, then remove from the heat and taste for seasoning.

4 Drain the pasta and turn it into a warmed bowl. Pour the sauce over the pasta and toss well. Serve, with salad and the Pecorino handed separately.

Ricotta & Chilli with Black Pasta

Serves 4

INGREDIENTS
300 g/11 oz dried black
   (squid ink) pasta
60 ml/4 tbsp very fresh ricotta cheese
60 ml/4 tbsp extra virgin olive oil
1 small fresh red chilli, seeded and
   finely chopped
1 small handful fresh basil leaves
salt and ground black pepper

1 Cook the pasta in salted boiling water according to the instructions on the packet until *al dente.* Meanwhile, put the ricotta in a bowl, season to taste and use a little of the hot water from the pasta pan to mix it to a creamy consistency. Taste for seasoning.

2 Drain the pasta. Heat the oil gently in the clean pan and add the pasta with the chilli and salt and pepper to taste. Toss quickly over a high heat to combine.

3 Divide the pasta equally among four warmed bowls, then top with the ricotta. Sprinkle with the basil leaves and serve immediately. Each diner tosses their own portion of pasta and cheese.

Right: Ricotta & Chilli with Black Pasta (top); Gorgonzola with Paglia e Fieno.

Gorgonzola with Paglia e Fieno

Serves 4

INGREDIENTS
275 g/10 oz dried paglia e fieno
25 g/1 oz/2 tbsp butter
5 ml/1 tsp finely chopped fresh sage or
   2.5 ml/½ tsp dried sage, plus fresh sage
   leaves to garnish (optional)
115 g/4 oz *torta di Gorgonzola* cheese, diced
45 ml/3 tbsp mascarpone cheese
75 ml/5 tbsp milk
50 g/2 oz/½ cup walnut halves, ground
30 ml/2 tbsp grated Parmesan cheese
salt and ground black pepper

1 Cook the pasta in salted boiling water according to the instructions on the packet until *al dente.* Meanwhile, melt the butter in a large pan over a low heat, add the sage and stir. Add the *torta di Gorgonzola* and mascarpone. Stir until the cheeses start to melt. Pour in the milk and keep stirring.

2 Sprinkle in the walnuts and Parmesan and add black pepper. Stir over a low heat until the mixture forms a creamy sauce. Do not allow it to boil, and do not cook the sauce for longer than a few minutes.

3 Drain the pasta and mix with the sauce. Garnish with sage, if you wish, and serve, with pepper ground on top.

Sun-dried Tomato Pesto with Linguine

Tomato pesto was once a rarity, but is becoming increasingly popular. To make it, sun-dried tomatoes are used instead of basil. The result is absolutely delicious. The pesto can also be used to flavour other dishes.

Serves 4

INGREDIENTS
25 g/1 oz/¼ cup pine nuts
25 g/1 oz/⅓ cup grated Parmesan cheese
50 g/2 oz/½ cup sun-dried tomatoes in olive oil
1 garlic clove, roughly chopped
60 ml/4 tbsp olive oil
350 g/12 oz fresh or dried linguine
salt and ground black pepper
basil leaves, to garnish
coarsely shaved Parmesan cheese, to serve

3 With the machine running, gradually add the olive oil through the feeder tube until it has all been incorporated evenly and the ingredients have formed a smooth-looking paste.

1 Put the pine nuts in a small, non-stick frying pan and toss over a low to medium heat for 1–2 minutes or until lightly toasted and golden.

2 Tip the nuts into a food processor. Add the grated Parmesan, sun-dried tomatoes and garlic, with pepper to taste. Process until finely chopped.

4 Cook the pasta in salted boiling water according to the packet instructions until *al dente*. Drain well, reserving a little of the cooking water.

5 Tip the pasta into a warmed bowl, add the pesto and a few spoonfuls of the hot water and toss well to combine. Serve immediately, garnished with basil leaves. Hand around the Parmesan shavings separately.

COOK'S TIP: You can make this pesto up to 2 days in advance and keep in the refrigerator. Pour a thin film of olive oil over the pesto, then cover with clear film (plastic wrap).

Alfredo's Fettuccine

This simple recipe was named after its inventor, a Roman restaurateur called Alfredo who devised the dish for a famous American actor.

Serves 4

INGREDIENTS
50 g/2 oz/¼ cup unsalted butter
200 ml/7 fl oz/scant 1 cup *panna da cucina* or double (heavy) cream
50 g/2 oz/⅔ cup grated Parmesan cheese, plus extra to serve
350 g/12 oz fresh fettuccine
salt and ground black pepper

1 Melt the butter in a large saucepan. Add the cream and bring it to the boil. Simmer for 5 minutes, stirring, then add the Parmesan, with salt and pepper to taste, and turn off the heat under the pan.

2 Cook the pasta in salted boiling water according to the instructions on the packet until *al dente*. Drain well.

3 Turn on the heat under the pan of cream to low, add the pasta all at once and toss until it is coated in the sauce. Taste for seasoning. Serve, with extra grated Parmesan offered separately.

Ham & Mascarpone with Linguine

Rich mascarpone cheese, Parmesan and milk combine to make a smooth, creamy sauce in this delicious dish.

Serves 6

INGREDIENTS
25 g/1 oz/2 tbsp butter
150 g/5 oz/scant ¾ cup mascarpone cheese
90 g/3½ oz cooked ham, cut into thin strips
30 ml/2 tbsp milk
45ml/3 tbsp grated Parmesan cheese,
    plus extra to serve
500 g/1¼ lb/5 cups fresh linguine
salt and ground black pepper

1 Gently melt the butter in a saucepan, add the mascarpone, ham and milk and stir until the mascarpone has melted. Add 15 ml/1 tbsp of the Parmesan and stir well.

2 Cook the pasta in salted boiling water according to the instructions on the packet until *al dente*. Drain thoroughly reserving a few tablespoons of the cooking water.

3 Tip the cooked pasta into a warmed bowl. Mix the reserved pasta cooking water into the sauce. Pour the sauce over the pasta, add the remaining grated Parmesan and toss well to combine thoroughly.

4 Taste for seasoning and serve the pasta immediately, with more ground pepper and extra grated Parmesan offered separately.

Saffron Sauce with Spaghetti

An easy dish, great for an impressive supper with a touch of luxury.

Serves 4

INGREDIENTS
350 g/12 oz dried spaghetti
a few saffron strands
30 ml/2 tbsp water
150 g/5 oz cooked ham, cut
    into matchsticks
200 ml/7 fl oz/scant 1 cup *panna da cucina*
    or double (heavy) cream
50 g/2 oz/⅔ cup grated Parmesan cheese,
    plus extra to serve
2 egg yolks
salt and ground black pepper

1 Cook the pasta in salted boiling water according to the instructions on the packet until *al dente.*

2 Meanwhile, put the saffron strands in a saucepan, add the water and bring to the boil immediately. Remove the pan from the heat and leave to stand for a while.

3 Add the ham to the pan containing the saffron. Stir in the cream and Parmesan, with a little salt and pepper to taste. Heat gently, stirring all the time. When the cream starts to bubble around the edges, remove the sauce from the heat and beat in the egg yolks.

4 Drain the cooked pasta and tip it into a large warmed bowl. Pour the sauce over the pasta and toss well. Serve immediately, with extra grated Parmesan offered separately.

Pesto with Eliche

Create perfect fresh pesto in moments using your food processor or blender.

Serves 4

INGREDIENTS

50 g/2 oz/1⅓ cups fresh basil leaves, plus
    extra to garnish
2–4 garlic cloves
60 ml/4 tbsp pine nuts
120 ml/4 fl oz/½ cup extra virgin olive oil
115 g/4 oz/1⅓ cups grated Parmesan cheese
25 g/1 oz/¼ cup grated Pecorino cheese
400 g/14 oz/3½ cups dried eliche
salt and ground black pepper
coarsely shaved Parmesan cheese, to serve

1 Put the first three ingredients in a blender or food processor. Add 60 ml/ 4 tbsp of the olive oil. Process, then stop the machine, remove the lid and scrape down the sides of the bowl.

2 Turn the machine on again and slowly pour the remaining oil in a thin, steady stream through the feeder tube. You may need to stop the machine and scrape down the sides of the bowl once or twice to make sure everything is evenly mixed.

3 Scrape the mixture into a large bowl and beat in the cheeses with a wooden spoon. Taste and add salt and pepper if necessary.

4 Cook the pasta in salted boiling water according to the instructions on the packet until *al dente*. Drain, then add to the bowl of pesto and toss well. Serve immediately, garnished with basil leaves. Offer shaved Parmesan separately.

Tuna Sauce with Farfalle

This simple-to-prepare dish makes a good weekday supper if you have canned tomatoes and tuna in the store cupboard. You could use white vermouth instead of the wine.

Serves 4

INGREDIENTS

30 ml/2 tbsp olive oil
1 small onion, finely chopped
1 garlic clove, finely chopped
400 g/14 oz can chopped Italian
   plum tomatoes
45 ml/3 tbsp dry white wine
8–10 pitted black olives, cut
   into rings
10 ml/2 tsp chopped fresh oregano or
   5 ml/1 tsp dried oregano, plus extra fresh
   oregano to garnish
400 g/14 oz/3½ cups
   dried farfalle
175 g/6 oz can tuna in olive oil
salt and ground black pepper

1 Heat the olive oil in a medium saucepan, add the onion and garlic and fry gently for 2–3 minutes until the onion is soft and golden.

2 Add the Italian chopped tomatoes and bring to the boil, then add the dry white wine and simmer for 2 minutes.

3 Stir in the black olives and fresh or dried oregano, with salt and ground black pepper to taste, then cover the pan tightly with a lid and cook gently for 20–25 minutes, stirring from time to time.

4 Meanwhile, cook the pasta in salted boiling water according to the instructions on the packet until *al dente*.

5 Drain the canned tuna and flake it roughly with a fork. Add the tuna to the sauce with about 60 ml/4 tbsp of the water used for cooking the pasta. Taste and adjust the seasoning.

6 Drain the cooked pasta well and tip it into a large warmed serving bowl. Pour the tuna sauce over the top and toss thoroughly to mix. Serve the dish immediately, garnished with sprigs of oregano.

Smoked Salmon with Linguine

Mushrooms, fresh dill and chives balance the richness of smoked salmon.

Serves 6

INGREDIENTS

30 ml/2 tbsp olive oil

115 g/4 oz/1½ cups button (white) mushrooms, finely sliced

250 ml/8 fl oz/1 cup dry white wine

7.5 ml/1½ tsp fresh dill or 5 ml/1 tsp dried dill

handful of fresh chives, snipped, plus extra whole chives to garnish

300 ml/½ pint/1¼ cups fromage frais

225 g/8 oz smoked salmon, cut into thin strips

lemon juice

350 g/12 oz/3 cups fresh linguine or spaghetti

sea salt and ground black pepper

1 Heat the oil in a wide, shallow pan. Add the mushrooms and fry for 4–5 minutes until softened.

2 Pour the wine into the pan. Increase the heat and boil for about 5 minutes until the wine has evaporated.

3 Stir in the herbs and fromage frais. Fold in the salmon and reheat, but do not let the sauce boil. Stir in pepper and lemon juice to taste. Cover the pan and keep the sauce warm.

4 Cook the pasta in salted boiling water according to the packet instructions until *al dente*. Turn into a serving dish and toss with the sauce before serving, garnished with chives.

Tuna & Anchovies with Spaghetti

This recipe from Capri — *Spaghetti alla Caprese* — is fresh and full of flavour.

Serves 4

INGREDIENTS
300 g/11 oz dried spaghetti
30 ml/2 tbsp olive oil
6 ripe Italian plum tomatoes, chopped
5 ml/1 tsp granulated (white) sugar
50 g/2 oz can anchovies in olive oil, drained
about 60 ml/4 tbsp dry white wine
200 g/7 oz can tuna in olive oil, drained
50 g/2 oz/½ cup pitted black olives,
    quartered lengthways
125 g/4¼ oz packet mozzarella cheese,
    drained and diced
salt and ground black pepper
fresh basil leaves, to garnish

1 Cook the pasta in salted boiling water according to the instructions on the packet until *al dente.*

2 Meanwhile, heat the oil in a medium saucepan. Add the tomatoes, sugar and pepper to taste, and toss over a medium heat for a few minutes until the tomatoes soften and the juices run.

3 Using kitchen scissors, snip a few anchovies at a time into the pan of tomatoes. Add the wine, tuna and olives and stir to mix evenly into the sauce.

4 Add the mozzarella and heat through without stirring. Taste and add salt if necessary.

5 Drain the pasta and tip it into a warmed bowl. Pour the sauce over, toss gently and sprinkle with basil leaves. Serve immediately.

Salmon & Prawns with Spaghetti

A lovely, fresh-tasting dish, perfect for an al fresco meal in summer.

Serves 4

INGREDIENTS

300 g/11 oz salmon fillet
200 ml/7 fl oz/scant 1 cup dry white wine
a few fresh basil sprigs, plus extra leaves
to garnish
6 ripe Italian plum tomatoes, peeled and
finely chopped
150 ml/¼ pint/⅔ cup double (heavy) cream
350 g/12 oz fresh or dried spaghetti
115 g/4 oz/⅔ cup peeled cooked prawns
(shrimp), thawed and dried, if frozen
salt and ground black pepper

1 Put the salmon skin-side up in a wide, shallow pan. Pour the wine over, then add the basil sprigs and seasoning.

2 Bring to the boil, cover and simmer gently for no more than 5 minutes. Lift the fish out of the pan and set aside to cool a little.

3 Add the tomatoes and cream to the liquid remaining in the pan and bring to the boil. Stir well, lower the heat and simmer, uncovered, for 10–15 minutes. Meanwhile, cook the pasta in salted boiling water according to the packet instructions until *al dente.*

4 Flake the fish into chunks, discarding the skin and bones. Add the fish and prawns to the sauce and heat through. Season to taste. Drain the pasta, mix with the sauce and serve with basil.

Prawns & Vodka with Paglia e Fieno

The unusual mixture of prawns and vodka makes a superb pasta sauce.

Serves 4

INGREDIENTS
30 ml/2 tbsp olive oil
¼ large onion, finely chopped
1 garlic clove, crushed
30 ml/2 tbsp sun-dried tomato purée (paste)
200 ml/7 fl oz/scant 1 cup *panna da cucina*
   or double (heavy) cream
350 g/12 oz fresh or dried paglia e fieno
12 raw tiger prawns (shrimp), peeled and
   chopped
30 ml/2 tbsp vodka
salt and ground black pepper

1 Heat the oil in a saucepan, add the onion and garlic and cook gently, stirring, for 5 minutes until softened.

2 Add the tomato purée and stir for 1–2 minutes, then add the cream and bring to the boil, stirring. Season to taste and let the sauce bubble until it starts to thicken slightly. Remove from the heat.

3 Cook the pasta in salted boiling water according to the instructions on the packet. When it is almost *al dente,* add the prawns and vodka to the sauce and toss quickly over a medium heat for 2–3 minutes until the prawns turn pink.

4 Drain the pasta and tip it into a warmed bowl. Pour the sauce over and toss well. Serve immediately.

25

Clam Sauce with Spaghetti

Known as *Spaghetti alle Vongole,* this is one of Italy's most famous dishes. It is a classic example of Venetian cooking.

Serves 4

INGREDIENTS
1 kg/2¼ lb fresh clams, well scrubbed
60 ml/4 tbsp olive oil
45 ml/3 tbsp chopped fresh
    flat-leaf parsley
120 ml/4 fl oz/½ cup dry white wine
350 g/12 oz dried spaghetti
2 garlic cloves
salt and ground black pepper

1 Discard any clams that are open and do not close when sharply tapped. Heat half the oil in a large pan, add the clams and 15 ml/1 tbsp of the parsley and cook over a high heat for a few seconds. Pour in the wine, cover and cook for about 5 minutes, shaking the pan frequently, until the clams have opened and cooked. Discard any clams that remain closed once cooked.

2 Meanwhile, cook the pasta in salted boiling water according to the instructions on the packet until *al dente.*

COOK'S TIP: This dish is also known as 'white clam sauce' to distinguish it from that other classic, 'clams in tomato sauce', which is popular in southern Italy.

3 Using a slotted spoon, transfer the clams to a bowl, discarding any that have failed to open. Strain the liquid and set it aside. Put 12 clams in their shells to one side for the garnish, then remove the rest from their shells.

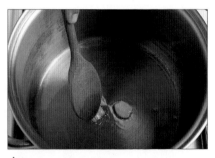

4 Heat the remaining oil in the clean pan. Fry the whole garlic cloves over a medium heat until golden, crushing them with the back of a spoon. Remove the garlic with a slotted spoon and discard.

5 Add the shelled clams to the oil remaining in the pan, gradually add some of the strained liquid from the clams, then add plenty of pepper. Cook for 1–2 minutes, gradually adding more liquid as the sauce reduces. Add the remaining parsley and cook for 1–2 minutes.

6 Drain the pasta thoroughly, add it to the pan and toss well. Turn into warmed individual dishes, scooping the shelled clams from the bottom of the pan and placing some of them on top of each serving. Garnish with the reserved clams in their shells and serve immediately.

Pink & Green Sauce with Farfalle

Pink prawns and green courgettes combine prettily with pasta bows.

Serves 4

INGREDIENTS

50 g/2 oz/¼ cup butter

2–3 spring onions (scallions), very thinly sliced on the diagonal

350 g/12 oz courgettes (zucchini), thinly sliced on the diagonal

60 ml/4 tbsp dry white wine

300 g/11 oz/scant 3 cups dried farfalle

75 ml/5 tbsp crème fraîche

225 g/8 oz/1⅓ cups peeled cooked prawns (shrimp), thawed and thoroughly dried if frozen

15 ml/1 tbsp roughly chopped fresh marjoram or flat-leaf parsley, or a mixture, to garnish

salt and ground black pepper

1 Melt the butter in a saucepan, add the onions and cook gently, stirring, for about 5 minutes until softened. Add the courgettes, with seasoning to taste, and stir-fry for 5 minutes. Pour over the wine and let it bubble, then cover and simmer for 10 minutes.

2 Cook the pasta in plenty of salted boiling water according to the instructions on the packet until *al dente*. Add the crème fraîche to the sauce and simmer, uncovered, for 10 minutes.

3 Add the prawns to the sauce, heat through and taste for seasoning. Drain the pasta, mix in the sauce and serve immediately, sprinkled with the herbs.

Squid Sauce with Black Pasta

Serve this tasty sauce with pasta appropriately coloured with squid ink.

Serves 4

INGREDIENTS
105 ml/7 tbsp olive oil
2 shallots, chopped
3 garlic cloves, crushed
45 ml/3 tbsp chopped fresh parsley
675 g/1½ lb cleaned squid, cut into rings and rinsed
150 ml/¼ pint/⅔ cup dry white wine
400 g/14 oz can chopped tomatoes
2.5 ml/½ tsp dried chilli flakes or powder
450 g/1 lb black tagliatelle
salt and ground black pepper

1 Heat the oil in a saucepan and add the shallots. Cook until pale golden, then add the garlic.

2 When the garlic colours a little, add 30 ml/2 tbsp of the parsley, stir, add the squid and stir again. Cook for 3–4 minutes, then add the wine.

3 Simmer for a few seconds, add the tomatoes, chilli flakes or powder and salt and pepper to taste. Cover and simmer gently for about 1 hour until the squid is tender. Add a little water if necessary.

4 Cook the pasta in salted boiling water according to the instructions on the packet until *al dente*. Drain and return to the pan. Add the sauce to the pasta and toss well. Divide among four bowls, sprinkle with the remaining parsley and serve at once.

Shellfish Sauce with Trenette

This typical Genoese sauce is ideal for a dinner-party dish.

Serves 4

INGREDIENTS

45 ml/3 tbsp olive oil
1 small onion, finely chopped
1 garlic clove, crushed
½ fresh red chilli, seeded and chopped
200 g/7 oz can chopped plum tomatoes
30 ml/2 tbsp chopped fresh flat-leaf parsley
400 g/14 oz fresh clams, well scrubbed
400 g/14 oz fresh mussels, well scrubbed
60 ml/4 tbsp dry white wine
400 g/14 oz/3½ cups dried trenette
a few fresh basil leaves
115 g/4 oz/⅔ cup peeled cooked prawns
    (shrimp), thawed and dried if frozen
salt and ground black pepper
chopped fresh herbs and lemon wedges,
    to garnish

2 In a large saucepan, heat the remaining olive oil. Add the clams and mussels with the rest of the flat leaf parsley and toss over a high heat for a few seconds. Pour in the dry white wine, then cover tightly. Cook for about 5 minutes, shaking the pan frequently, until the clams and mussels have opened.

3 Remove the pan from the heat and, using a slotted spoon, transfer the clams and mussels to a bowl, discarding any shellfish that have failed to open.

4 Strain the cooking liquid into a measuring jug and set aside. Reserve eight clams and four mussels in their shells for the garnish, then remove the rest from their shells.

1 Heat 30 ml/2 tbsp of the oil in a saucepan. Add the onion, garlic and chilli and cook over a medium heat for 1–2 minutes, stirring. Stir in the tomatoes, half the parsley and pepper to taste. Bring to the boil, lower the heat, cover and simmer for 15 minutes.

COOK'S TIP: Before cooking the clams and mussels, any that are open should be sharply tapped. Discard them if they fail to close, as they are not safe for eating.

5 Cook the pasta in salted boiling water according to the instructions on the packet until *al dente*. Meanwhile, add 120 ml/4 fl oz/½ cup of the reserved seafood liquid to the tomato sauce. Bring to the boil over a high heat, stirring. Lower the heat, tear in the basil leaves and mix in the prawns with the shelled clams and mussels. Heat through, then taste for seasoning.

6 Drain the cooked pasta and tip it into a large warmed serving bowl. Add the seafood sauce and toss well to combine. Serve in individual bowls, sprinkle with herbs and garnish each portion with a lemon wedge, two reserved clams and one mussel in their shells.

Lobster with Capelli d'Angelo

This is a stylish dish for a special occasion. If you're feeling really extravagant, replace the sparkling wine with champagne.

Serves 4

INGREDIENTS

meat from the body, tail and claws of
  1 cooked lobster
juice of ½ lemon
40 g/1½ oz/3 tbsp butter
4 fresh tarragon sprigs, leaves stripped
  and chopped, plus extra to garnish
60 ml/4 tbsp double (heavy) cream
90 ml/6 tbsp sparkling dry white wine
60 ml/4 tbsp fish stock
300 g/11 oz/scant 3 cups fresh
  capelli d'angelo
salt and ground black pepper
about 10 ml/2 tsp lumpfish roe,
  to garnish (optional)

1 Cut the lobster meat into small pieces and put it in a bowl. Sprinkle with the lemon juice to prevent the lobster meat from discolouring.

2 Melt the butter in a large saucepan, add the lobster meat and tarragon and stir over the heat for a few seconds.

3 Add the cream and stir for a few seconds more, then pour in the wine and stock, with salt and pepper to taste. Simmer for 2 minutes, then remove from the heat and cover.

4 Cook the pasta in salted boiling water according to the instructions on the packet until *al dente*. Drain well, reserving a few spoonfuls of the cooking water.

COOK'S TIP: To remove the meat from a lobster, place the lobster on a board with its underbelly facing uppermost. With a large, sharp knife, cut the lobster in half lengthways. Spoon out the green liver and any pink roe (coral) and reserve these, then remove and discard the gravel sac (stomach). Pull the white tail meat out from either side of the shell and discard the black intestinal vein. Crack the claws with a nutcracker just below the pincers and remove the meat from the base. Pull away the small pincer, taking the white membrane with it, then remove the meat from this part of the shell. Pull the meat from the large pincer shell.

5 Place the pan of lobster sauce over a medium to high heat, add the pasta and toss for just long enough to combine and heat through; moisten with a little of the reserved water from the pasta. Serve immediately, sprinkled with lumpfish roe if you like and garnished with chopped tarragon.

33

Chicken, Broccoli & Cheese with Penne

Blue Gorgonzola cheese makes this sauce meltingly delicious.

Serves 4

INGREDIENTS

115 g/4 oz/scant 1 cup broccoli florets,
   divided into sprigs
50 g/2 oz/¼ cup butter
2 skinless chicken breast fillets, cut into
   thin strips
2 garlic cloves, crushed
400 g/14 oz/3½ cups dried penne
120 ml/4 fl oz/½ cup dry white wine
200 ml/7 fl oz/scant 1 cup *panna da cucina*
   or double (heavy) cream
90 g/3½ oz Gorgonzola cheese, rind removed
   and diced small
salt and ground black pepper
grated Parmesan cheese,
   to serve

1 Plunge the broccoli into salted boiling water and boil for 2 minutes, then drain and refresh under cold running water. Drain again and set aside.

2 Melt the butter in a saucepan and add the chicken and garlic, with seasoning. Fry for 3 minutes. Meanwhile, cook the pasta in salted boiling water according to the packet instructions. Add the wine and cream to the chicken and simmer, stirring, for about 5 minutes until the sauce has reduced. Add the broccoli and heat.

3 When the pasta is *al dente,* drain it and mix it into the sauce. Stir in the Gorgonzola. Serve with Parmesan.

Chicken & Cherry Tomatoes with Farfalle

Quick to prepare and easy to cook, this colourful dish is full of flavour.

Serves 4

INGREDIENTS
350 g/12 oz skinless chicken breast fillets,
    cut into bite-size pieces
60 ml/4 tbsp Italian dry vermouth
10 ml/2 tsp chopped fresh rosemary,
    plus 4 whole sprigs to garnish
15 ml/1 tbsp olive oil
1 onion, finely chopped
90 g/3½ oz piece Italian salami, diced
275 g/10 oz/2½ cups dried farfalle
15 ml/1 tbsp balsamic vinegar
400 g/14 oz can Italian cherry tomatoes
good pinch of crushed dried red chillies
salt and ground black pepper

1 Combine the chicken, vermouth, half the rosemary and seasoning.

2 Heat the oil in a saucepan, add the onion and salami and fry for about 5 minutes, stirring. Meanwhile, cook the pasta in salted boiling water according to the instructions on the packet until *al dente.*

3 Add the chicken and vermouth to the onion and salami and fry for 3 minutes or until the chicken is white on all sides. Add the vinegar, cherry tomatoes and dried chillies and simmer for a few minutes more. Taste the sauce for seasoning.

4 Drain the pasta and tip it into the sauce. Toss in the remaining chopped rosemary. Serve garnished with the sprigs of rosemary.

Tomato & Chilli Sauce with Penne

The Italian name for this sauce, *arrabbiata,* which literally translates as "enraged" or "furious", refers to the fiery quality of the chillies.

Serves 4

INGREDIENTS
25 g/1 oz dried porcini mushrooms
90 g/3½ oz/7 tbsp butter
150 g/5 oz pancetta or rindless smoked streaky (fatty) bacon, diced
1–2 dried red chillies, to taste
2 garlic cloves, crushed
8 ripe Italian plum tomatoes, peeled and chopped
a few fresh basil leaves, torn, plus extra to garnish
350 g/12 oz/3 cups fresh or dried penne
50 g/2 oz/⅔ cup grated Parmesan cheese
25 g/1 oz/⅓ cup grated Pecorino cheese
salt

1 Soak the dried mushrooms in warm water to cover for 15–20 minutes. Drain, then squeeze dry with your hands. Finely chop the mushrooms.

2 Melt 50 g/2 oz/¼ cup of the butter in a medium saucepan. Add the pancetta or bacon and stir-fry over a medium heat until golden and slightly crisp. Remove the pancetta with a slotted spoon and set it aside.

3 Add the mushrooms to the pan and cook in the same way. Remove and set aside with the pancetta or bacon.

4 Crumble one chilli into the pan, add the garlic and cook, stirring, for a few minutes until the garlic turns golden.

5 Add the tomatoes and basil and season with salt. Cook gently, stirring occasionally, for 10–15 minutes. Meanwhile, cook the pasta in salted boiling water according to the instructions on the packet until *al dente.*

6 Add the pancetta or bacon and the mushrooms to the sauce. Season to taste, adding more chillies if you prefer a hotter flavour. If the sauce is too dry, stir in a little of the pasta water.

7 Drain the pasta and tip it into a warmed bowl. Dice the remaining butter, add it to the pasta with the cheeses, then toss until well coated. Pour the tomato sauce over the pasta, toss well and serve immediately, with a few basil leaves sprinkled on top.

Pork with Rigatoni

An excellent meat sauce using minced pork rather than beef.

Serves 4

INGREDIENTS
25 g/1 oz/2 tbsp butter
30 ml/2 tbsp olive oil
1 small onion, finely chopped
½ carrot, finely chopped
½ celery stick, finely chopped
2 garlic cloves, finely chopped
150 g/5 oz minced (ground) pork
60 ml/4 tbsp dry white wine
400 g/14 oz can chopped Italian
    plum tomatoes
a few fresh basil leaves, plus extra
    to garnish
400 g/14 oz/3½ cups dried rigatoni
salt and ground black pepper
shaved Parmesan cheese,
    to serve

1 Heat the butter and oil in a large pan, add the chopped vegetables and cook, stirring frequently, for 3–4 minutes. Add the pork and cook gently for 5–6 minutes, stirring to break up any lumps of meat.

2 Add the wine, tomatoes, whole basil leaves and seasoning to taste. Bring to the boil, cover and simmer for 40 minutes, stirring occasionally.

3 Cook the pasta in salted boiling water according to the packet instructions until *al dente*. Add a ladleful or two of the cooking water to the sauce. Season. Drain the pasta, add it to the sauce and toss. Serve, garnished with basil and Parmesan.

Bresàola Sauce with Pasta

Here the almost gamy flavour of bresàola (cured beef) is used to good effect.

Serves 6

INGREDIENTS
30 ml/2 tbsp olive oil
1 small onion, finely chopped
150 g/5 oz bresàola, cut into thin strips
4 (bell) peppers (red and orange or yellow),
     seeded and diced
120 ml/4 fl oz/½ cup dry white wine
400 g/14 oz can chopped Italian
     plum tomatoes
450 g/1 lb/4 cups dried pasta tubes
50 g/2 oz/⅔ cup shaved Parmesan cheese
small handful of fresh basil leaves
salt and ground black pepper

1 Heat the oil in a saucepan and add the onion and bresàola. Cover and cook over a low heat for 5–8 minutes.

2 Add the peppers, wine, 5 ml/1 tsp salt and plenty of pepper. Stir well, then simmer for 10–15 minutes. Add the tomatoes and bring to the boil, stirring. Cover and simmer, stirring occasionally, for 20 minutes or until the sweet peppers are very soft and quite creamy.

3 Meanwhile, cook the pasta in a pan of salted boiling water according to the instructions on the packet until *al dente*.

4 Drain the pasta and tip it into a warmed bowl. Taste the sauce for seasoning, then pour it over the pasta and add half the Parmesan. Toss well then serve, sprinkled with the basil and the remaining Parmesan.

Spicy Sausage Sauce with Fusilli

Feel the heat with this sausage and tomato sauce, which combines with pasta spirals to make a really tasty dish from southern Italy.

Serves 4

INGREDIENTS
400 g/14 oz spicy pork sausages
30 ml/2 tbsp olive oil
1 small onion, finely chopped
2 garlic cloves, crushed
1 large yellow (bell) pepper, seeded and cut
    into strips
5 ml/1 tsp paprika
5 ml/1 tsp dried mixed herbs
5–10 ml/1–2 tsp chilli sauce
400 g/14 oz can Italian plum tomatoes
250–300 ml/8–10 fl oz/1–1¼ cups
    vegetable stock
300 g/11 oz/scant 3 cups fresh or
    dried fusilli
salt and ground black pepper
grated Pecorino cheese, to serve

2 Heat the oil in a large saucepan, add the onion and garlic and cook over a low heat, stirring frequently, for 5–7 minutes until soft. Add the yellow pepper, paprika, herbs and chilli sauce to taste. Cook gently for 5–7 minutes, stirring occasionally.

3 Tip in the tomatoes, breaking them up with a wooden spoon, then add salt and pepper to taste and stir well. Cook over a medium heat for 10–12 minutes, adding the vegetable stock gradually as the sauce reduces.

4 Add the sausage pieces to the sauce, reduce the heat to low and cook for 10 minutes. Meanwhile, cook the pasta in salted boiling water according to the instructions on the packet until *al dente*.

1 Grill the sausages for 10–12 minutes until browned on all sides. Drain on kitchen paper and cut diagonally into 1 cm/½ in pieces.

5 Taste the sauce for seasoning. Drain the pasta and add it to the pan of sauce. Toss well, then divide among four warmed bowls. Sprinkle each serving with a little grated Pecorino and serve immediately, with more Pecorino offered separately.

COOK'S TIP: There are two types of paprika. Spanish *pimenton dulce* is softer than the fiery Hungarian variety, so check the country of origin on the packet and adjust the quantity used to suit your taste.

Creamy Pea & Ham Sauce with Pipe Rigate

Prettily flecked with pink and green, this is a lovely dish for a spring or summer supper party. You could use fresh, cooked peas if available.

Serves 4

INGREDIENTS

25 g/1 oz/2 tbsp butter
15 ml/1 tbsp olive oil
150–175 g/5–6 oz/1¼–1½ cups frozen
   peas, thawed
1 garlic clove, crushed
150 ml/¼ pint/⅔ cup chicken stock, dry
   white wine or water
30 ml/2 tbsp chopped fresh flat-leaf parsley
175 ml/6 fl oz/¾ cup *panna da cucina* or
   double (heavy) cream
115 g/4 oz prosciutto crudo
   (Parma ham), shredded
350 g/12 oz/3 cups dried pipe rigate
salt and ground black pepper
chopped fresh herbs, to garnish

1 Melt half the butter with the olive oil in a medium saucepan until foaming. Add the thawed frozen peas and the garlic to the pan, followed by the chicken stock, wine or water.

2 Sprinkle in the chopped parsley and add salt and pepper to taste. Cook over a medium heat, stirring frequently, for 5–8 minutes or until most of the liquid has evaporated.

3 Add about half the cream, increase the heat to high and let the cream bubble, stirring constantly, until it thickens and coats the peas. Remove from the heat, stir in the prosciutto and taste for seasoning.

4 Cook the pasta in salted boiling water according to the instructions on the packet until *al dente*. Drain well.

VARIATION: Prosciutto is quite expensive, but it tastes very good in this dish. To cut the cost you could use ordinary cooked ham or pancetta but it will not have such a distinctive flavour.

5 Immediately melt the remaining butter with the rest of the cream in the pan in which the pasta was cooked. Add the pasta and toss over a medium heat until it is evenly coated.

6 Pour the sauce into the pan containing the pasta, toss lightly to combine and heat through. Serve immediately, sprinkled with fresh chopped herbs.

Pumpkin & Parmesan Sauce

The sweet flavour of pumpkins is nicely balanced by Parmesan cheese.

Serves 4

INGREDIENTS

800 g/1¾ lb fresh pumpkin flesh, cut
   into small cubes
65 g/2½ oz/5 tbsp butter
15 ml/1 tbsp olive oil
2 garlic cloves, crushed
75 g/3 oz/1½ cups fresh
   white breadcrumbs
300 g/11 oz tagliatelle
115 g/4 oz rindless smoked back
   bacon, diced
1 onion, sliced
150 ml/¼ pint/⅔ cup single (light)
   cream
50 g/2 oz/⅔ cup grated Parmesan cheese
freshly grated nutmeg
30 ml/2 tbsp chopped fresh flat-leaf parsley,
   plus whole sprigs to garnish
15 ml/1 tbsp snipped fresh chives
salt and ground black pepper

1 Bring a large saucepan of water to
the boil. Tip in the pumpkin cubes
and simmer for about 10 minutes until
just tender. Drain and set aside.

2 Melt two-thirds of the butter with
the oil in a frying pan. Add the garlic
and breadcrumbs. Fry gently until the
crumbs are golden brown and crisp.
Drain on kitchen paper and keep warm.

3 Cook the pasta in salted boiling
water according to the packet
instructions until *al dente*. Drain.

4 Heat the remaining butter and fry
the bacon and onion for 5 minutes.
Stir in the cream, bring to just below
boiling point, add the pasta and reheat.
Stir in the parmesan, nutmeg, parsley
and chives. Season. Serve, sprinkled
with the breadcrumbs and parsley.

Lamb & Sweet Pepper Sauce

This simple sauce can be served with either spaghetti or macaroni.

Serves 4–6

INGREDIENTS
60 ml/4 tbsp olive oil
250 g/9 oz lamb neck fillet, diced quite small
2 garlic cloves, finely chopped
2 bay leaves
250 ml/8 fl oz/1 cup dry white wine
4 ripe Italian plum tomatoes, peeled
  and chopped
2 large red (bell) peppers, seeded and diced
salt and ground black pepper
cooked pasta, to serve

1 Heat half the olive oil in a medium saucepan, add the pieces of lamb and sprinkle with a little salt and pepper.

2 Cook the meat over a medium to high heat for about 10 minutes, stirring often, until browned on all sides.

3 Sprinkle in the garlic and add the bay leaves, then pour in the wine and let it bubble until reduced. Add the remaining oil, the tomatoes and red peppers; stir to mix. Season again.

4 Cover the pan and simmer over a low heat for 45–55 minutes or until the lamb is very tender. Stir occasionally during cooking and moisten with water if the sauce becomes too dry. Remove the bay leaves from the sauce before serving it with pasta.

Bolognese Sauce with Tagliatelle

Bolognese sauce, the famous *ragù* from Bologna, is nowadays commonly served with spaghetti, but the traditional dish uses tagliatelle.

Serves 4

INGREDIENTS
30 ml/2 tbsp olive oil
1 onion, finely chopped
1 carrot, finely chopped
1 celery stick, finely chopped
1 garlic clove, crushed
350 g/12 oz minced (ground) beef
150 ml/¼ pint/⅔ cup red wine
250 ml/8 fl oz/1 cup milk
400 g/14 oz can chopped tomatoes
15 ml/1 tbsp sun-dried tomato purée (paste)
350 g/12 oz dried tagliatelle
salt and ground black pepper
shredded fresh basil, to garnish
grated Parmesan cheese, to serve

1 Heat the oil in a large saucepan. Add the onion, carrot, celery and garlic and cook gently, stirring frequently, for about 10 minutes until softened. Do not allow the vegetables to colour.

2 Add the minced beef and cook over a medium heat until the meat changes colour, stirring constantly and breaking up any lumps with a wooden spoon. Pour in the wine and stir frequently until it has evaporated.

3 Add the milk and continue cooking and stirring until this has evaporated.

4 Stir in the tomatoes and tomato purée, with salt and pepper to taste. Simmer the sauce, uncovered, over the lowest possible heat for at least 45 minutes.

5 Cook the pasta in salted boiling water according to the instructions on the packet until *al dente*. Drain thoroughly and tip into a large warmed bowl.

6 Pour the sauce over the pasta and toss to combine. Garnish with basil and serve at once, with Parmesan cheese handed separately.

COOK'S TIP: Don't skimp on the cooking time – it is essential for a full-flavoured Bolognese sauce. Some Italian cooks insist on cooking it for 3–4 hours, so the longer, the better.

Meatballs with Spaghetti

Meatballs simmered in a sweet and spicy tomato sauce are truly delicious with spaghetti. Children love them and you can easily leave out the chillies.

Serves 6–8

INGREDIENTS
350 g/12 oz minced (ground) beef
1 egg
60 ml/4 tbsp roughly chopped fresh
    flat-leaf parsley
2.5 ml/½ tsp crushed dried red chillies
1 thick slice white bread,
    crusts removed
30 ml/2 tbsp milk
about 30 ml/2 tbsp olive oil
300 ml/½ pint/1¼ cups passata
400 ml/14 fl oz/1⅔ cups
    vegetable stock
5 ml/1 tsp granulated (white) sugar
350–450 g/12 oz–1 lb fresh or
    dried spaghetti
salt and ground black pepper
shaved Parmesan cheese, to serve

1 Put the minced beef in a large bowl. Add the egg, half the parsley and a pinch of crushed chillies. Season with plenty of salt and pepper.

2 Tear the bread into small pieces and place in a small bowl with the milk. Leave to soak for a few minutes, then squeeze out the excess milk and crumble the bread over the meat mixture. Mix with a wooden spoon, then use your hands to knead the mixture so that it becomes smooth and quite sticky.

3 Wash your hands, rinse them under the cold tap, then pick up small pieces of the mixture and roll them between your palms to make about 40–60 small balls. Place the meatballs, in a single layer, on a tray and chill in the refrigerator for about 30 minutes.

4 Heat the oil in a large, non-stick frying pan. Cook the meatballs in batches until browned on all sides.

5 Pour the passata and vegetable stock into a large saucepan. Heat gently, then add the remaining crushed red chillies and the granulated sugar, with salt and freshly ground black pepper to taste. Add the meatballs, bring to the boil, cover and simmer for 20 minutes.

6 Cook the pasta in salted boiling water according to the packet instructions until *al dente*. Drain and tip into a large warmed bowl.

7 Pour the sauce over the pasta and toss gently. Sprinkle with the remaining parsley and serve with shaved Parmesan handed separately.

VARIATION: To ring the changes you could use pork instead of beef for these meatballs.

Fresh Tomato Sauce

This is the famous Neapolitan sauce, made in summer when tomatoes are ripe and sweet and fresh basil is plentiful.

Serves 4

INGREDIENTS
675 g/1½ lb ripe Italian plum tomatoes
60 ml/4 tbsp olive oil
1 onion, finely chopped
350 g/12 oz fresh or dried spaghetti
small handful of fresh basil leaves,
    finely shredded
salt and ground black pepper
coarsely shaved Parmesan cheese, to serve

1 With a sharp knife, cut a cross in the bottom (flower) end of each tomato. Plunge them into boiling water, leave for 30 seconds, then lift them out with a slotted spoon. Peel off the skin and roughly chop the flesh.

2 Heat the oil in a large saucepan, add the onion and cook over a low heat, stirring frequently, for about 5 minutes until softened. Add the tomatoes, with salt and pepper to taste. Cover and simmer, stirring occasionally, for 30–40 minutes until thick.

3 Meanwhile, cook the pasta in salted boiling water according to the instructions on the packet until *al dente*.

4 Remove the sauce from the heat, stir in the basil and taste for seasoning. Drain the pasta, tip it into a warmed bowl, pour the sauce over and toss well. Serve immediately, with shaved Parmesan offered separately.

Raw Tomato Sauce

The unusual combination of hot, freshly cooked pasta with the cold tomato sauce makes a deliciously refreshing dish for summer.

Serves 4

INGREDIENTS
500 g/1¼ lb ripe Italian
   plum tomatoes
large handful of fresh basil leaves
75 ml/5 tbsp extra virgin olive oil
115 g/4 oz ricotta salata cheese,
   diced
1 garlic clove, crushed
salt and ground black pepper
cooked pasta and coarsely shaved Pecorino
   cheese, to serve

1 Roughly chop the tomatoes, removing the cores and as many of the seeds as you can. Tear the basil leaves into shreds with your fingers.

2 Put all the ingredients (except thePecorino cheese) in a bowl, seasoning to taste, and stir well. Cover and leave at room temperature for 1–2 hours to let the flavours mingle.

3 Taste the sauce to check the seasoning before tossing it with hot, freshly cooked pasta and the ricotta salata. Serve immediately with shavings of Pecorino offered separately.

COOK'S TIP: This sauce goes well with most kinds of pasta, whether long or short. Ensure that you use only the ripest tomatoes for the best results.

Sun-dried Tomatoes & Radicchio with Paglia e Fieno

This is a light, modern dish that will impress friends and family.
Its attractive presentation belies the ease with which it is prepared.

Serves 4

INGREDIENTS
45ml/3 tbsp pine nuts
350 g/12 oz dried paglia e fieno
45 ml/3 tbsp extra virgin olive oil
30 ml/2 tbsp sun-dried tomato purée (paste)
2 pieces sun-dried tomatoes in olive oil,
   drained and cut into very thin slivers
40 g/1½ oz radicchio leaves,
   finely shredded
4–6 spring onions (scallions), thinly sliced
   into rings
salt and ground black pepper

1 Put the pine nuts in a non-stick
frying pan and toss over a low heat
until they are lightly toasted and
golden. Remove and set aside.

2 Cook the pasta in salted boiling
water according to the packet
instructions until *al dente,* keeping the
colours separate by using two pans.

COOK'S TIP: If you find the
presentation too fiddly, you can toss
the sun-dried tomato and radicchio
mixture with the pasta in one large
warmed bowl before serving, then
serve it sprinkled with the spring
onions and toasted pine nuts.

3 Meanwhile, heat 15 ml/1 tbsp of
the oil in a medium saucepan. Add the
sun-dried tomato purée and tomatoes,
then stir in 150 ml/¼ pint/⅔ cup of
the water used for cooking the pasta.
Simmer until the sauce is slightly
reduced, stirring constantly.

4 Mix in the shredded radicchio, then
taste and season if necessary. Keep on a
low heat. Drain the pasta, keeping the
colours separate, and return to their
cooking pans. Add 15 ml/1 tbsp oil to
each pan and toss over a medium to
high heat until the pasta is glistening.

5 Arrange a portion of green and white pasta in the two halves of each of four warmed bowls, then spoon the tomato and radicchio mixture in the centre of each bowl.

6 Sprinkle the spring onions and toasted pine nuts decoratively over the top and serve immediately. Before eating, each diner should toss the sauce ingredients with the pasta to mix well.

Asparagus & Cream with Garganelli

A lovely recipe for late spring when bunches of fresh young asparagus are on sale in shops and markets everywhere.

Serves 4

INGREDIENTS

1 bunch fresh young asparagus, about
    250–300 g/9–11 oz
350 g/12 oz/3 cups dried garganelli
25 g/1 oz/2 tbsp butter
200 ml/7 fl oz/scant 1 cup *panna da cucina*
    or double (heavy) cream
30 ml/2 tbsp dry white wine
90–115 g/3½–4 oz/1–1⅓ cups grated
    Parmesan cheese
30 ml/2 tbsp chopped fresh mixed herbs,
    such as basil, flat-leaf parsley, chervil,
    marjoram and oregano
salt and ground black pepper

1 Trim off and throw away the woody ends of the asparagus – after trimming, you should have about 200 g/7 oz asparagus spears. Cut the spears diagonally into pieces that are roughly the same length and shape as the garganelli.

2 Blanch the asparagus spears in salted boiling water for 2 minutes, the tips for 1 minute. Immediately after blanching, drain the asparagus, rinse in cold water and set aside.

3 Cook the pasta in salted boiling water according to the instructions on the packet until *al dente.*

4 Meanwhile, put the butter and cream in a medium saucepan, add salt and pepper to taste and bring to the boil. Simmer for a few minutes until the cream reduces and thickens, then stir in the asparagus, wine and about half the Parmesan. Taste for seasoning and keep on a low heat.

5 Drain the pasta and tip it into a warmed bowl. Pour the sauce over the pasta, sprinkle with the fresh herbs and toss well. Serve immediately, topped with the remaining Parmesan.

Wild Mushroom Sauce with Fusilli

A very rich dish with an earthy flavour and lots of garlic, this makes an ideal main course for vegetarians.

Serves 4

INGREDIENTS
150 g/5 oz canned wild mushrooms
    in olive oil
25 g/1 oz/2 tbsp butter
225 g/8 oz/3 cups fresh wild mushrooms,
    sliced if large
5 ml/1 tsp finely chopped
    fresh thyme
5 ml/1 tsp finely chopped fresh
    marjoram or oregano, plus extra
    herbs to serve
4 garlic cloves, crushed
350 g/12 oz/3 cups fresh or
    dried fusilli
200 ml/7 fl oz/scant 1 cup *panna da cucina*
    or double (heavy) cream
salt and ground black pepper

1 Drain about 15 ml/1 tbsp of the oil from the mushrooms into a medium saucepan. Slice or chop the bottled mushrooms into bite-size pieces, if they are large.

COOK'S TIP: When tossing pasta with a sauce, use two large spoons or a large spoon and fork. Lift the pasta fairly high and swirl it around, ensuring that every piece is coated evenly in the sauce.

2 Add the butter to the oil in the pan and place over a low heat until sizzling. Add all the mushrooms, the herbs and garlic, with seasoning to taste. Simmer over a medium heat, stirring frequently, for about 10 minutes or until the fresh mushrooms are lightly browned.

3 Meanwhile, cook the pasta in salted boiling water according to the instructions on the packet until *al dente.*

4 As soon as the mushrooms are cooked, increase the heat to high and toss the mixture with a wooden spoon to drive off any excess liquid. Pour in the cream and bring to the boil, stirring, then taste and add more salt and pepper if needed.

5 Drain the pasta and tip it into a warmed bowl. Pour the sauce over the pasta and toss well. Serve immediately, sprinkled with extra fresh herb leaves.

Vegetable Medley Sauce

A medley of tasty vegetables, combined with melted butter and olive oil.

Serves 4

INGREDIENTS
2 carrots
1 courgette (zucchini)
75 g/3 oz green beans
1 small leek
2 ripe Italian plum tomatoes
handful of fresh flat-leaf parsley
25 g/1 oz/2 tbsp butter
45 ml/3 tbsp extra virgin olive oil
2.5 ml/½ tsp granulated (white) sugar
115 g/4 oz/1 cup frozen peas
salt and ground black pepper
cooked pasta, to serve

1 Dice the carrots and courgette finely. Top and tail the green beans, then cut them into 2 cm/¾ in lengths. Slice the leek thinly. Peel and dice the tomatoes. Chop the parsley and set aside.

2 Melt the butter in the oil in a medium saucepan. When the mixture sizzles, add the prepared leek and carrots. Sprinkle the sugar over and fry, stirring frequently, for about 5 minutes.

3 Stir in the courgette, green beans, peas and plenty of salt and pepper. Cover tightly and cook over a low to medium heat for 5–8 minutes until the vegetables are tender, stirring occasionally to prevent sticking.

4 Stir in the parsley and tomatoes, heat through and adjust the seasoning to taste. Serve at once, tossed with freshly cooked pasta of your choice.

VARIATION: You could use broad beans instead of French beans.

Aubergines with Spaghetti

This famous dish, *Spaghetti alla Bellini,* is named after the Sicilian composer.

Serves 4–6

INGREDIENTS

60 ml/4 tbsp olive oil
1 garlic clove, roughly chopped
450 g/1 lb ripe Italian plum tomatoes, peeled
    and chopped
vegetable oil, for shallow frying
350 g/12 oz aubergines (eggplant), diced
    small
400 g/14 oz fresh or dried spaghetti
handful of fresh basil leaves, shredded
115 g/4 oz ricotta salata cheese,
    coarsely grated
salt and ground black pepper

1 Heat the olive oil, add the garlic and cook gently for 1–2 minutes. Stir in the tomatoes, then add salt and pepper to taste. Cover and simmer for 20 minutes.

2 Meanwhile, pour oil into a deep frying pan to a depth of about 1 cm/ ½ in. Heat until hot but not smoking, then fry the aubergines in batches for 4–5 minutes until lightly browned. Remove the aubergines with a slotted spoon and drain on kitchen paper.

3 Cook the pasta in salted boiling water according to the packet instructions until *al dente.* Meanwhile, stir the fried aubergines into the tomato sauce and warm through. Taste for seasoning.

4 Drain the pasta and tip it into a warmed bowl. Add the sauce, basil and a generous handful of the cheese. Toss well and serve with the remaining cheese sprinkled on top.

Slow-cooked Onions & Cabbage with Pasta

Meltingly tender, sweet onions, lightly cooked greens still retaining a slight crunch and toasted pine nuts combine in this unusual and colourful vegetarian pasta sauce.

Serves 4

INGREDIENTS

25 g/1 oz/2 tbsp butter
15 ml/1 tbsp extra virgin olive oil, plus more
    for drizzling (optional)
500 g/1¼ lb Spanish onions, halved and
    thinly sliced
5–10 ml/1–2 tsp balsamic vinegar
400 g/14 oz cavolo nero, spring
    greens, kale or Brussels sprout
    tops, shredded
400–500 g/14 oz–1¼ lb/3½–5 cups dried
    pasta (such as penne or fusilli)
75 g/3 oz/1 cup grated
    Parmesan cheese
50 g/2 oz/½ cup pine nuts, toasted
salt and ground black pepper

1 Heat the butter and olive oil together in a large frying pan. Stir in the onions, coating them in the butter mixture. Cover and cook very gently, stirring occasionally, for 20 minutes until the onions are very soft.

COOK'S TIP: Toast pine nuts in a dry frying pan for 2 minutes, turning frequently, or in a preheated medium oven for 2-3 minutes. Put on a timer as the nuts burn easily.

2 Uncover the pan and continue to cook the onions gently until they have turned golden yellow. Add the balsamic vinegar and season well with salt and pepper, then cook for a further 1–2 minutes. Set aside.

3 Blanch the cavolo nero, spring greens, kale or Brussels sprout tops in lightly salted, boiling water for about 3 minutes. Drain well, pat dry with kitchen paper, and add to the onions, then cook over a low heat for about 3–4 minutes.

4 Cook the pasta in plenty of salted boiling water according to the packet instructions until *al dente*. Drain well, then add to the pan of onions and greens and toss thoroughly to mix.

5 Season well with salt and freshly ground black pepper and stir in half the grated Parmesan. Transfer the pasta to warmed plates. Scatter the pine nuts and more Parmesan on top and serve the dish immediately, offering more olive oil for drizzling over to taste.

VARIATIONS: You could use toasted walnuts instead of pine nuts. This dish would also work well with grated Pecorino cheese instead of Parmesan. Choose a mature variety such as romano for the strongest flavour.

Artichokes with Penne

Richly flavoured with garlic, this sauce uses the tender hearts of globe artichokes with the distinctive aniseed flavour of fennel.

Serves 6

INGREDIENTS
juice of ½–1 lemon
2 globe artichokes
30 ml/2 tbsp olive oil
1 small fennel bulb, thinly sliced, with
    feathery tops reserved
1 onion, finely chopped
4 garlic cloves, finely chopped
handful of fresh flat-leaf parsley,
    roughly chopped
400 g/14 oz can chopped Italian
    plum tomatoes
150 ml/¼ pint/⅔ cup dry white wine
350 g/12 oz/3 cups dried penne
10 ml/2 tsp capers, chopped
salt and ground black pepper
grated Parmesan cheese, to serve

1 Have ready a bowl of cold water to which you have added the juice of ½ lemon. Cut off the artichoke stalks, then discard the outer leaves until the pale inner leaves that are almost white at the base remain.

2 Cut off the tops of these leaves so that the base remains. Cut the base in half lengthways, then prise the hairy choke out of the centre with the tip of the knife and discard. Cut the artichokes lengthways into 5 mm/¼ in slices, adding them immediately to the bowl of acidulated water.

3 Bring a large saucepan of water to the boil. Add a good pinch of salt, then drain the artichokes and add immediately to the pan. Boil for 5 minutes, drain and set aside.

4 Heat the oil in a deep frying pan and add the fennel, onion, garlic and parsley. Cook, stirring frequently, for about 10 minutes until the fennel has softened and is lightly coloured.

5 Add the tomatoes and wine, with salt and pepper to taste. Bring to the boil, stirring, then cover and simmer for 10–15 minutes. Stir in the artichokes, replace the lid and simmer for 10 minutes more.

6 Meanwhile, cook the pasta in plenty of salted boiling water according to the packet instructions until *al dente*.

7 Drain the cooked pasta, reserving a little of the cooking water. Stir the chopped capers into the artichoke and fennel sauce, then taste for seasoning and add the remaining lemon juice if you like a lightly piquant flavour.

8 Tip the pasta into a large warmed bowl, pour the sauce over and toss well to mix, adding a little of the reserved cooking water if you prefer a runnier sauce. Serve immediately, garnished with the reserved fennel fronds. Hand around a bowl of grated Parmesan separately.

Index

This edition is published by Lorenz Books,
an imprint of Anness Publishing Ltd,
108 Great Russell Street, London WC1B 3NA info@anness.com

www.lorenzbooks.com; www.annesspublishing.com

© Anness Publishing Limited 2014

If you like the images in this book and would like to investigate
using them for publishing, promotions or advertising, please visit
our website www.practicalpictures.com for more information.

Publisher: Joanna Lorenz
Editor: Valerie Ferguson & Helen Sudell
Series Designer: Bobbie Colgate Stone
Designer: Andrew Heath
Production Controller: Steve Lang

Recipes contributed by: Michelle Berriedale-Johnson,
Angela Boggiano, Carla Capalbo, Jacqueline Clark, Maxine
Clark, Roz Denny, Brian Glover, Jenni Wright

Photography: Edward Allwright, James Duncan,
Michelle Garrett, John Heseltine, Amanda Heywood,
Janine Hosegood, William Lingwood

A CIP catalogue record for this book is available from the
British Library

COOK'S NOTES

Bracketed terms are intended for American readers.

For all recipes, quantities are given in both metric and imperial
measures and, where appropriate, in standard cups and spoons.
Follow one set of measures, but not a mixture, because they are
not interchangeable.

Standard spoon and cup measures are level. 1 tsp = 5ml,
1 tbsp = 15ml, 1 cup = 250ml/8fl oz. Australian standard
tablespoons are 20ml. Australian readers should use 3 tsp
in place of 1 tbsp for measuring small quantities.

American pints are 16fl oz/2 cups. American readers should use
20fl oz/2.5 cups in place of 1 pint when measuring liquids.

Electric oven temperatures in this book are for conventional
ovens. When using a fan oven, the temperature will probably
need to be reduced by about 10–20°C/20–40°F. Since ovens
vary, you should check with your manufacturer's instruction
book for guidance.

Medium (US large) eggs are used unless otherwise stated.

PUBLISHER'S NOTE:
Although the advice and information in this book are believed
to be accurate and true at the time of going to press, neither the
authors nor the publisher can accept any legal responsibility or
liability for any errors or omissions that may have been made nor
for any inaccuracies nor for any loss, harm or injury that comes
about from following instructions or advice in this book.